Working at the Post Office

Learning to Subtract Two Three-Digit Numbers Without Regrouping

Barbara M. Linde

Rosen Classroom Books & Materials
New York

With special thanks to Jan Weiner, Postmaster, Yorktown, Virginia, and Michelle Smith, Postmaster, Ochopee, Florida.

Published in 2004 by The Rosen Publishing Group, Inc.
29 East 21st Street, New York, NY 10010

Book Design: Haley Wilson

Photo Credits: Cover © Jeffery Sylvester/FPG International; p. 5 (post office) © Richard Bickel/Corbis; pp. 5 (interior of post office), 12 © Mark Gibson/Index Stock; p. 7 © Nik Wheeler/Corbis; p. 8 (top image) © Ted Horowitz/Corbis; p. 8 (inset) © Kindra Clineff/Index Stock; p. 11 © Lawrence Migdale/Stock Boston/PictureQuest; p. 11 (inset) © Jeff Dunn/Index Stock.

ISBN: 0-8239-8855-4
6-pack ISBN: 0-8239-7339-5

Manufactured in the United States of America

Contents

Subtracting at the Post Office

Most cities and towns have a post office. The workers at the post office make sure the mail gets to the right place. Some workers sort the mail. Some workers take the mail to different places. Other workers sell stamps. Workers use math skills like subtraction to figure out the number of letters that are sorted and **delivered**, or the amount of change to give to a **customer**.

Mail that is brought to the post office is put into large
bins to be sorted.

The Largest and Smallest Post Offices

Chicago has the largest post office in the United States. The building is 14 stories high. This post office gets millions of pieces of mail every day. Hundreds of people work there.

The nation's smallest post office is in Ochopee (oh-CHOP-ee), Florida. Only 2 people work there. The Ochopee Post Office gets about 600 letters a day in winter and about 300 letters a day in summer. How many fewer letters does it get each day in the summer than it gets each day in the winter?

600 letters each day in winter
−300 letters each day in summer

300 fewer letters each day in summer

The post office receives 300 fewer letters each day in the summer than it does each day in the winter.

The Ochopee Post Office was once used as a place to store tools before it became a post office in 1953.

Some sorting clerks use special machines that
sort the mail by zip codes.

The Sorting Clerk

Mail is brought to the post office in mail trucks. All of the mail is sorted. **Sorting clerks** put letters and **magazines** into cases for the mail carriers. A carrier's case has a space for each address on the mail **route**. The clerks work very quickly. They can sort as many as 600 pieces of mail in 1 hour!

On Monday, Mrs. Jones sorted 752 magazines. On Tuesday, she sorted 898 magazines. How many more magazines did she sort on Tuesday than on Monday?

898 magazines sorted on Tuesday
−752 magazines sorted on Monday
146 more magazines sorted on Tuesday

Mrs. Jones sorted 146 more magazines on Tuesday than she did on Monday.

The Mail Carrier

Mail carriers start work early in the morning. Each carrier has a route to follow. Before they leave the post office, the carriers put the mail in the order of the street addresses on their route.

Mr. Ross delivers mail to 958 apartments. Ms. Hale delivers mail to 742 houses. How many fewer deliveries does Ms. Hale make?

$$
\begin{array}{r}
958 \\
-742 \\
\hline
216
\end{array}
$$

958 Mr. Ross's deliveries
−742 Ms. Hale's deliveries
216 fewer deliveries

Ms. Hale makes 216 fewer deliveries than Mr. Ross.

Mail carriers work outside all day in the rain, the snow, and the sun. Some mail carriers walk their route. They carry bags full of mail. Other carriers drive small trucks.

Counter clerks work in the front of the post office.
They can tell you how much it will cost to send a
package to a friend in another city.

The Counter Clerk

Counter clerks work in the front part of the post office. They sell stamps and weigh **packages**. A counter clerk can answer questions about how long a letter will take to reach a certain place. Counter clerks take in money for stamps and make change for customers. It's important for counter clerks to know how to add and subtract.

One customer gave Mrs. Sanchez $3.80 for 10 stamps that cost a total of $3.70. How much change did the customer get back?

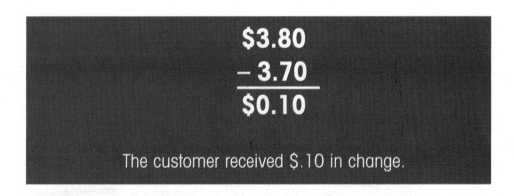

$$\begin{array}{r} \$3.80 \\ -\ 3.70 \\ \hline \$0.10 \end{array}$$

The customer received $.10 in change.

The Postmaster

The **postmaster** is in charge of the post office. The postmaster helps customers with any problems they may have and makes sure the mail goes out on time. The postmaster uses subtraction to figure out problems like this: The post office sends 256 letters out by truck. It sends 141 letters by airplane. How many more letters will go out by truck?

> **256** letters sent by truck
> **−141** letters sent by airplane
> **115** more letters sent by truck
>
> The post office sends 115 more letters out by truck than by airplane.

When you get mail, think about the math skills that post office workers must know to do their jobs.

Glossary

counter clerk (KOWN-tuhr KLERK) A person who sells stamps and weighs packages at the post office.

customer (KUHS-tuh-muhr) Someone who buys goods or services.

deliver (dih-LIH-vuhr) To take something to someone.

magazine (MA-guh-zeen) A journal of true or make-believe stories that are written by different people. Magazines may come out weekly, monthly, or yearly.

package (PA-kij) A box of things.

postmaster (POST-mass-tuhr) The person in charge of the post office.

route (ROOT) The places a mail carrier delivers the mail.

sorting clerk (SOHR-ting KLERK) A person who puts the mail in order by zip codes.

Index